Clean Hands, Dirty Hands

Sing Along
Tune: Row, Row, Row Your Boat

Jo Cleland

Rourke
Educational Media

rourkeeducationalmedia.com

Teacher Notes available at
rem4teachers.com

www.rourkeeducationalmedia.com

PHOTO CREDITS: Cover: © Eric Limón; page 3: © zhang bo; page 4: © Jorge Salcedo; page 5: © Bidouze Stéphane; page 6: © Olga Altunina; page 7: © Matt Antonino; page 8: © Kim Gunkel; page 9: © Daniel Laflor; page 10: © Ana Abejon; page 11: © Steve Debenport; page 12: © jo unruh; page 13: © Sang Lei; page 14: © Franky De Meyer; page 15: © Arthur Carlo Franco; page 16: © Percent; page 17: © Pipa100; page 18: Katseyephoto; page 19: © kali9; page 20: © Michelle Gibson; page 21: © Omikron960

Editor: Precious McKenzie

Cover Design by Tara Raymo
Page Design by Mikala Collins

Library of Congress PCN Data

Clean Hands, Dirty Hands / Jo Cleland
(Sing and Read, Healthy Habits, K-2)
ISBN 978-1-61810-080-1 (hard cover)(alk. paper)
ISBN 978-1-61810-213-3 (soft cover)
Library of Congress Control Number: 2011944389

Rourke Educational Media
Printed in the United States of America,
North Mankato, Minnesota

rourkeeducationalmedia.com

customerservice@rourkeeducationalmedia.com • PO Box 643328 Vero Beach, Florida 32964

Dig, dig, dig in mud.
Dirty, dirty hands.

3

Wash, wash, wash with **soap**.

Now you have clean hands.

Crawl, crawl, crawl on the floor.
Dirty, dirty hands.

Wash, wash, wash with soap.

Now you have clean hands.

Climb, climb, climb a tree.
Dirty, dirty hands.

Wash, wash, wash with soap.

Now you have clean hands.

Catch, catch, catch a ball.

Dirty, dirty hands.

Wash, wash, wash with soap.

Now you have clean hands.

Scratch, scratch, scratch the dog.

Dirty, dirty hands.

Wash, wash, wash with soap.

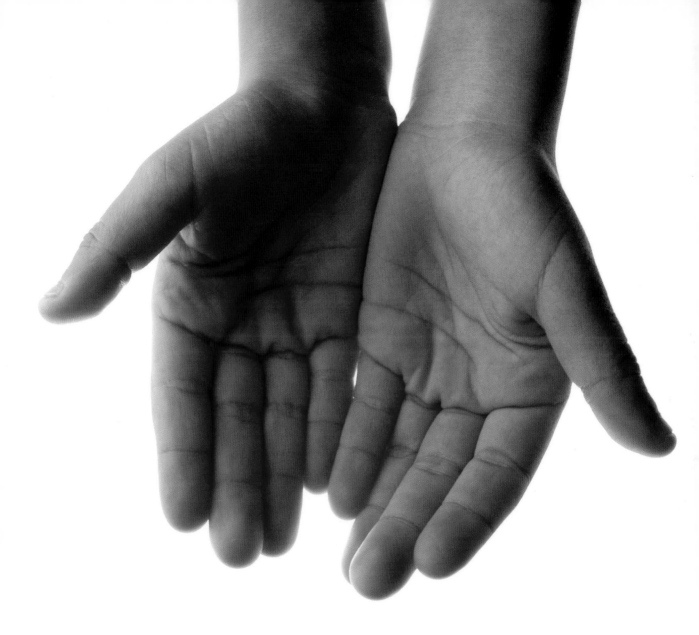

Now you have clean hands.

Glossary

catch (KACH): to grab something moving through the air

crawl (KRAWL): to move on your hands and knees

dirty (DURT-ee): not clean

scratch (SCRACH): to scrape with your nails

soap (SOHP): a substance used for cleaning

wash (WOSH): to clean with soap and water

Clean Hands, Dirty Hands

Tune: Row, Row, Row Your Boat

Dig, dig, dig in mud.
Dirty, dirty hands.
Wash, wash, wash with soap.
Now you have clean hands.

Crawl, crawl, crawl on the floor.
Dirty, dirty hands.
Wash, wash, wash with soap.
Now you have clean hands.

Climb, climb, climb a tree.
Dirty, dirty hands.
Wash, wash, wash with soap.
Now you have clean hands.

Catch, catch, catch a ball.
Dirty, dirty hands.
Wash, wash, wash with soap.
Now you have clean hands.

Scratch, scratch, scratch the dog.
Dirty, dirty hands.
Wash, wash, wash with soap.
Now you have clean hands.

Index

Websites

www.scrubclub.org/site/meet.aspx

kidshealth.org/kid/talk/qa/wash_hands.html#cat20086

www.ehow.com/list_6868976_children_s-art-activities-washing-hands.html

About the Author

Jo Cleland enjoys writing books, composing songs, and making games. She loves to read, sing, and play games with children.

Ask The Author!
www.rem4students.com

24